Henry Doman

**Songs of Lymington**

Henry Doman

**Songs of Lymington**

ISBN/EAN: 9783337007317

Printed in Europe, USA, Canada, Australia, Japan

Cover: Foto ©Thomas Meinert / pixelio.de

More available books at **www.hansebooks.com**

# SONGS OF LYMINGTON,

BY

HENRY DOMAN,

AUTHOR OF "THE CATHEDRAL AND OTHER POEMS."

LONDON:
SIMPKIN, MARSHALL, & Co.
SALISBURY: BROWN & Co., CANAL.
LYMINGTON: H. DOMAN.
1867.

## ERRATA.

Page 36, line 5, read—" The day WENT down."

Page 72, line 1, read—" In this fair scene not OUT of place."

Page 164, line 15, read—" And SINK forgotten in the shade."

# INDEX.

| | |
|---|---:|
| Lymington | page 1 |
| The Waning Year | 4 |
| A Garden Thought | 7 |
| Here and There | 12 |
| Sunset | 18 |
| The Nightingale | 21 |
| England's Glory | 24 |
| The Lost Friend | 28 |
| Time | 30 |
| Memory | 35 |
| Sing, O River | 39 |
| The Bride | 43 |
| Molly and I | 45 |
| God's Hill | 48 |
| Maggie Blake | 52 |
| Lilies of the Valley | 55 |
| The Ball | 57 |

| | |
|---|---:|
| The Gift of Flowers | page 61 |
| The Street and the River | 65 |
| The Fancy Ball (Newlands) | 69 |
| The Wave | 73 |
| The Old Church Organ | 75 |
| My Lady's Place | 84 |
| Long Ago | 87 |
| The Last Minstrel | 91 |
| Evermore | 98 |
| Sunday Morning | 101 |
| Night | 107 |
| The Sleepless Night | 108 |
| The Coming of the King | 111 |
| Hurst Castle | 119 |
| Franky Brown | 124 |
| The Spectres of Buckland Rings | 127 |
| Leila (A Memorial) | 130 |
| Fiddlers' Race | 134 |
| The Groaning Tree of Baddesley | 139 |
| The Seven Brothers | 143 |
| The Singer in the Valley | 147 |
| Thou Renewest the Face of the Earth | 150 |

| | |
|---|---:|
| The Saxon Relic in Romsey Abbey ..*page* | 154 |
| Talk o' th' Hill | 159 |
| Not Yet | 162 |
| The House Minstrel | 165 |
| Ellen Somers | 169 |
| The Pestilence | 171 |
| The Captain's Wife | 175 |
| The Wreck of the "London" | 179 |
| The Forest Nook | 184 |
| The Grave by the River | 187 |
| The Seer | 190 |

# THE SECOND VOLUME.

*A year or two ago into the world*
*An unpretentious book of song I sent,*
*Much fearing such bold emprise to repent.*
*Some look'd upon't with mighty scorn, and curled*
*Disdainful lips, loud wondering what was meant*
*By such presumption; some, to mercy bent,*
*Suspended judgment, read, and gave it place*
*With nobler volumes; some there were indeed,*
*Who praised it slightly for poetic grace*
*And promise in the future, though not much:*
*And there were some who in those rhymes the touch*
*Of minstrel true discerned, and bade me sing*
*Again in mine own fashion: unto such,*
*Embolden'd, I another offering bring.*

*A wreath of melodies, that many cares*
*And sorrows of a graver cast, have made*
*Dear to the singer, singing in the shade*
*Of a cold world: some psalms it hath, and prayers,*
*A few low symphonies and solemn airs,*
*Stray gleams of fancy, broken thoughts that play*
*Round memory's misty mountains, still and grey;*
*Here shade and shine commingle, nature's scenes*
*Lie mirror'd in the music, fair and clear;*
*And if some note of sadness intervenes,*
*To move the tender heart, and ask a tear—*
*Are there not clouds to dim the brightest day?*
*Forgive such tribute to the lost and dear—*
*A few names that I loved, remembered here,*
*And left, enshrined in song, along my way.*

## LYMINGTON:

### TO —

---

Beautiful is Lymington,
   Terraced by the sea:
Queenly from her wooded steep,
She looks down upon the deep,
Where on shining beaches leap
   Waves exultingly.

Stately, about Lymington,
   Rise the forests grand:

Mighty trunk and mossy limb,
Vast, innumerable, dim,
Shadow many a river's brim,
    Wandering through the land.


Fair lieth Lymington,
    Listening to the sweet
Song the merry lark doth make,
Singing for sweet singing's sake:
Every note that falls, a flake
    Of music, at her feet.


Pleasant paths hath Lymington,
    Flowery ways, and fair;
Shelter'd glades and sunny fields,
Shades wherein the mavis builds,
Slopes the dying sunset gilds
    With heav'nly glories rare.

Maidens sweet hath Lymington,
    Stately men and tall:
But the fairest thing to me
Is the friend she gave; and he
Ever to my heart shall be,
    The dearest of them all.

Songs are these of Lymington,
    In spare moments sung:
These a poet's gift I make;
These I ask of you to take,
For sweet love, and for the sake
    Of days when we were young.

# THE WANING YEAR.

"Let us weep for the waning year!"
  I heard three sorrowful voices say:
The first was a robin singing clear,
The second a wind that hover'd near,
The third a river, through meadows drear,
  Travelling its lonely way.

"Weep, weep!" the robin he said:
  "The days are dreary; the night is cold;
The fruits have fallen; the leaves are shed;

## THE WANING YEAR.

The lily hath withered; the rose is dead;
There's a pall of snow in the garden spread
 For the year so grey and old."


"Weep, weep!" sang the mourning wind,
 A voice in the tree-tops bare and high,
Where the pale green ivy sits entwined,
And mistletoe gleams on the oaken rind;
" Weep for the year so old and blind;
 The year that is near to die."


"Weep,"—sang the river—"weep to-day!"
 And the willows wept by the sobbing shore:
And golden shallow and sandy bay
To the sworded sedge and rushes grey,
 Said, "Weep for the friend that must pass away;
 The year we shall see no more."

The voices sad rang a sorrowful chime,
   Mournful and sweet to a poet's ear;
My soul with the cadence was beating time,
And memory wept for a vanish'd prime,
And I wove the music into a rhyme—
   And a song for the dying year.

## A GARDEN THOUGHT.

If kind looks had but power
On tree, and herb, and flower,
   How would my garden bloom!
Could I, whene'er I please,
Bid the soft southern breeze
Bring balm here and perfume,
How would my roses glow:
How fairest buds would blow:
How would their spices flow
   Beneath that summer sky!

## A GARDEN THOUGHT.

Black blight should flee away,
Nor caterpillar slay,
Nor festering mildew stay;
   Nor beauty ever die.


Each wind that came should kiss
Ivy and clematis,
   Whose leaves should toy and twine
With fragrant flowering bean,
And honeysuckles green,
   Round ev'ry bow'r of mine.
Pansies of velvet jet,
With polyanthus set;
Primrose and mignonette;
   Should blossom where I went:
Clove and carnation red,
For me should ever shed
   Their soul-reviving scent.

## A GARDEN THOUGHT.

The snowdrop all the year
Should bare her bosom clear,—
A saint, to God most dear:
   Each primrose that came up
Should never, never fade,
But an immortal maid,
   Should from her golden cup,
Drink sweet dews as they fall
From Eden's crystal wall.
Fair lilies white and tall
   Should all my borders grace:
And king-cup and jonquil,
Myrtle and daffodil,
Should, through all changes, still
   Have here their dwelling place.


Through all the flying hours,
I'd have my garden bow'rs

Crown'd with undying flowers:
And in their pleasant shade,
Should summer music ring;
Here the dark merle should bring
His tales of love and spring;
And songs by angels made,
The tenderer mavis sing.
And when the day grew pale,
Then should the nightingale
Flood all the listening vale
With her sweet sorrowing.
Beauty should never fly,
Nor love, nor melody.


Ah me! how vain the thought!
Yet in my fancy, not
Without some comfort fraught,—
Some glimpse of that pure lore

And wisdom from above,
Instinct with light and love,
That God's white-winged Dove
   Brings to this earthly shore.
May not a gentle face,
And tender words of grace,
Bring into every place
   A glory and a spell,
That shall with magic rare,
Make human gardens fair,
Where all is bleak and bare,
   Where evil passions dwell?
Oh love! oh tender light,
That makest darkness bright!
Who shall declare thy might?
   Who shall thy magic tell?

## HERE AND THERE.

When the Sabbath noon of rest
    Crowns the many-laboured week,
They who know and love us best
    Have not very far to seek,
Would they find my wife and me
Sitting with our children three.
Yet we have six darlings fair;
Three are here, and three are there:
          Here and there!

Three have left a world of sin;
   Little pilgrims soon at home:
Early privileg'd to win
   That for which we longer roam.
Three fair scions of our race
Still give life its tender grace;
Three whom death's cold hand did
    spare,
Three are here, and three are there:
        Here and there!


It is on such hallow'd noons,
   They come clustering round my
     knees,
Singing holy hymns and tunes,—
   Little, simple melodies.
Then we count them, one by one;
Two sweet daughters, a dear son:

Six there were; the sum is clear:
Three are there, and three are here:
>There and here.

As a miser sadly tells
  Golden pieces that are few;
As the night on silent dells
  Slowly droppeth silver dew;
So we count them—so we weep,
Inly mourning; grief lies deep:
Though the face a calm may wear,
Thoughts will wander here and there;
>Here and there!

Yet in grieving we are glad;
  Comfort mingles with our sighs;
Two fair daughters, one bright lad;
  These, with their clear-shining eyes,
Tender, loving, trusting, true,

Spread o'er life a rosy hue,

Rainbows set in clouds of care :

Rainbows are not needed there ;

    Here, not there !


There !—where death has never crept ;

 There !—where trouble never falls ;

There !—where tears are never wept ;

 Sin no more the soul appals :

Through the radiant gates that shine

Golden, oh thou wife of mine !

Darlings three in death most dear,

Early pass'd ; and three are here :

    There, and here !


So upon these stated times,

 From some pressing care releas'd,

On our ears the tender chimes

 Falling, we prepare a feast :

Nuts, that make a sober show,
Oranges of golden glow,
Apple ruddy, mellow pear,
Spread for darlings here, not there;
    Here, not there!

These we take and pour the wine;
 Then on memory's voyage bound,
While the little faces shine,
 Tiny glasses make their round.
Tiny glass to tiny lip;
Tiny tipplers take a sip;
One bright boy, two daughters fair,
Softly lisping,—"here and there!"
    "Here, and there!"

"Here, and there!"—the words are said:
Only two of five can tell

What is by the toast conveyed,—
   What its hidden, soothing spell.
Yet we prize the blessed grief;
Would not ask a day's relief;
Bind it to us with a prayer,
Blending ever, "here with there."
                . Here, and there!

Here, and there; and there, and here!
   On two worlds our spirits look :
Earth is lovely : heav'n is dear.
   Like the Angel of the Book,
Foot on ocean, foot on land,
So our souls divided stand.
Earth is holy; heaven is fair;
Children here, and children there!
                Here, and there!

## SUNSET.

Slowly, proudly, bear him to his grave
  In the western sea :
Lay his fading beams along the wave ;
Beams that made the morn so fair and brave,
When his golden sword the darkness clave ;
  When, serene and free,
Came the daylight from her crystal cave,
And through heav'n her flaming chariots drave
  In royal pageantry.

Music sighing, waileth in the trees:
    Tender, dying falls
Fill the air, and mingle with the sea's
Sterner, deeper, grander melodies:
Ocean-harpings wander with the breeze:
    Cloudy, golden palls
Dusky, hang along the palaces,
Where from earth the sadden'd gazer sees
    Glory's broken walls.

Oh, ye clouds, that bear his mighty hearse!
    Trail your crimson plumes!
Sing a dirge, sing dirges in sad verse,
Mountain winds that moan through all your firs!
Bend, oh woods! and your green heads immerse
    In deepest shades and glooms:
Sing a dirge, sing dirges; and rehearse
All his majesty whom Night inters
    Within her place of tombs.

Sing a dirge, sing dirges; oh ye waves,
> To your mountains hoar!

Wander, wailing, weeping, through your caves.

Sob, oh sea, above thy many graves!

Gleam again, oh dying light that paves
> Ocean's western floor!

Gleam again, oh light upon the waves!

"Lo, the day is dead!"—the night wind raves,—
> "Dead for evermore!"

## THE NIGHTINGALE.

—

When the day hath sunk to sleep,
   And the moon, all pure and pale,
Through the sky, a queen doth sweep,
Where the planets blink and peep:
In the valley green and deep,—
   " Weep,—weep ! "—
     Weeps the nightingale.

Stars are shining on the deep,
   Lighting up a lonely sail:
All on board save one asleep:
He is left the watch to keep:
Breezes bring to him the " weep,—
   Weep,—weep!"—
   Of the nightingale.


Dark and dim the shadows creep
   O'er the dwellings in the vale,
Round the castle's broken keep,
And the crags along the steep:
Through the silence comes the "weep,—
   Weep,—weep!"—
   Of the nightingale.


And my darling lies asleep:
   Very still her face, and pale:

Dim the lines that round it creep;

And her slumber is so deep,

That I cannot choose but weep,—

   Weep,—weep!—

   With the nightingale.

# ENGLAND'S GLORY.

Thy glory standeth, England, at the full:
A sun, in whose meridian splendour fades
The light of Greece or Rome; whose brightness
    shades
All other: a great country, in whose rule
Half this old planet rests—the other hopes.
Star of the nations through the deepening years!
Fair is thy shield and radiant: none shall shame
The land that freedom to the world endears.

Science and song for thee,—arts, arms,—unfold
Each day an ampler page, a wider fame.
The blessing of great Solomon is thine,
In majesty and wisdom, pow'r and gold;
And thine the stores of plenty; corn and wine.
God stands, as Joshua, on the purple slopes
Of history—bids the light of thy renown
To shine with increase never to go down.

For God, thy God, hath long anointed thee
With joy above thy fellows; and hath set
Thee in the place where many thrones have met;
And giv'n thee all the kingdoms of the sea,
The riches of the land, the master-key
Of commerce, and the tolls of all the world.
His hand hath sprinkled thee with the pure salt
That loseth not its savour,—many-pearled.
In that red emblem on thy flag, unfurled
In equatorial climes, on polar snows,

East, west, or north,—the terror of thy foes;
Its glory spreading without break or halt,
Bounded alone by fair creation's arch,—
We trace the secret of thy mighty march.

Art thou not the king's daughter, fair within,
And clad in glorious garments, golden-wrought?
Are not fair truth, faith, honor, duty,—brought
To thee,—sweet sisters of thy race and kin?
Are not thy children princes, born to win
Fame for all love of great deeds, and high thought,
And noble emprise? Do not the distress'd
Of the wide world find refuge near thy feet?
Thou mother of the weary, art thou not
The patriot's mother, home, and place of rest?
Do not th' eternal waves, that round thee beat,
Sing thee of all lands loveliest and best—
The beauteous realm—the pearl of the blue sea—
The priceless gem o' the world, by God confess'd:

Beneath whose flag the chainéd slave grows free?
He touches liberty who touches thee.

The crested billows breaking on thy rocks,
These are thy watch-dogs, surly in their play,
Faithful to thee; in their unruly way
Guarding thy shores, and shaking their green locks
And great sea-manes by every cliff and bay.
The organ-winds, whose anthems clash and roll
With peals of storm and glory through the skies,
These are thy choristers, whose voices rise
Chanting to Him whose mighty hands control
Creation—who hath made thee great and wise.
Thus guarded, thus besung, lo! thou dost sit
A queen of nations, girdled with the sea,
And crown'd with many crowns; yet, as is fit,
Wearing them all for Him who gave them all to
    thee.

## THE LOST FRIEND.

A friend I had: I lov'd him well:
  None dearer to my heart could be:
But in that heart there tolls a bell
  Of death; for he is dead—to me.

At church and market still his talk
  Is heard: he wanders by the sea:
In busy streets he's known to walk:
  Yet he is but a ghost—to me.

## THE LOST FRIEND.

He died some time ago: that is,
   His truth expired, as it might be;
And friendship's lamp was broken: this
   Is fact, that he is dead—to me.

His death was sudden, like the flame
   Of lightning falling in the sea:
Grim falsehood, the foul murderer, came,
   And slew him dead—that is, to me.

I wept for him, as those who weep
   For losses that eternal be:
I laid him in a grave so deep,
   He'll never more come back—to me.

I carv'd his name above the grave
   With bitter grief, lamentingly;
For I was fool, and he was knave,
   And my old friend is dead—to me.

## TIME.

There is a silent foe that steals,
    Day after day,
    Our goods away:
We may not hear his horses' heels;
His chariot rolls on noiseless wheels;
His ear is deaf to all appeals:
    In vain we pray—
    "Let Friendship stay!
Oh, give to Love a long delay!"

To other hearts his heart he steels;
With equal hands he sternly deals;
 He smites to slay:
 And visions gay,
 And glory's ray,
And love and friendship—where are they?


He spreads green moss on stately walls;
He planteth in ancestral halls
 Seeds that shall play,
 And swing, and sway,
In leaves that wave where ruin calls;
Where, stone from stone, the building
 falls;
And through each crevice ivy crawls:
Where, open to the night and day,
Old splendours sink in slow decay,
And terror the lone heart appals.

All to his cruel touch must yield:
>> He weareth down
>> The helm, the crown,
The cross on knighthood's sculptured
>> shield:
He laughs at legends of renown;
He treats the monarch as the clown.


He steals her beauty from the fair:
>> Her grace and pride
>> He skulks beside:
He bends her stately form with care.
With silver sprinkles, here and there,
He dims her glorious flowing hair:
He wrinkles all her maiden bloom;
He scores her brow with lines of doom:
He takes the lustre from her eyes,
Youth's pearly tints, and vermeil dyes;

He cools affection, true and tried:
Alike with bridegroom and with bride,
His cruel, cruel fingers dare
To break the knot that love hath tied,
That God hath own'd and sanctified.


He makes a thousand pleasures fade:
He lives our dearest hopes to kill:
At every turn of life's long hill,
He waits in deadly ambuscade.
    His plans are made;
    His snares are laid:
And death, obedient to his will,
Stands ready,—waiting, waiting still.
He sweeps the nations like the leaves
Of autumn, when the wind is high:
He sees all generations die:
He binds dead centuries in sheaves.

He lifteth up nor voice nor cry,
Through endless years
Of smiles and tears;
A silent reaper, pausing never.
By mortal griefs untouch'd, unstirred;
With stealthy hand, unseen, unheard,
He reapeth, reapeth on for ever!

## MEMORY.

The soul may wander in a country fair,
   That is more fair than bright;
A country that is neither here nor there;
Whose bounds are boundless, stretching every-
     where.
   It hath a tender light,
A world of sorrowful beauty, and an air
Of home; it giveth to the raptured sight
Things that have faded, forms that were most dear:
Therein sweet voices fall upon the ear,
   Long silent in death's night:
It hath the blooming fields, the water'd glades,
The old church pathway through the woodland
     shades;

It keeps the love that we have lost; it holds
The buds of life the crimsons and the golds,
And glories with which God did deck the skies,
When in the dying west,
The day when down with awful pageantries,
And the green earth had rest:
When all things beauteous had a living tongue:
The hallow'd, halcyon days when we were young.



It hath its churches and cathedrals dim,
    And bells of mellow sound;
Service, and sacred song, and requiem,
    And consecrated ground;
Wherein the dearest things we had are laid,
But not for ever, as in this cold earth,
Where death hath an eternal silence made,
    And keeps his prisoners bound.

There love may live again, and truth, and worth:
They hear us in their graves; they are not dead:
They only rest; and answering to our call,
They come as we have known them from our birth:—
The sire, with reverent head;
The mother, laden with her cares for all;
The long-lost, long-wept little ones that fled
Like summer birds departing ere their time;
Bright manhood, stricken down in early prime;
And holy maids, white lilies of the Lord,
Lifting clear hands above us with the blessing
Of peace. The dead wife comes to us restored
In beauty; soothes the heart with love's caressing,
Kisses away the gathering tears that tell
Of grief; and brings a calm ineffable.


It is a hallowed land,
Shaded with tenderness, and rounded off

With sorrow. They alone may understand
Its sweetness, who have sorrowed. They who scoff
At tears, when love hath suffer'd, may not dwell
Therein, nor touch its shore, nor breathe its calm.
There is a mighty swell
Of waves along its border all must pass:
A troublous voyage: he who loveth well
Rides through wild waters to a "sea of glass;"
Then lands, and gathers, as he travels, balm:
A wanderer, travel-weary, tempest-toss'd,
Finding again the treasures he had lost.

Where is this peaceful strand,
Whose light has never shone on earth or sea?
Tell us, oh poet, where this land may be.

The light is that of sorrow, and the land
Is Memory!

## SING, O RIVER!

Sing, O river!
  To thy dewy meads,
Where green sedges quiver
  'Mid the whispering reeds.
Where the willow lowly weeps
O'er thy crystal flowing deeps;
Where the golden lily sleeps,
    Sing, O river!
    Sing!

Sing, O river!
> Where in pleasant dells,
Nature hangeth over
> Buds and broider'd bells.
Tender fragrance there is made,
Where within the leafy shade,
Roses bloom and roses fade:
>> Sing, O river!
>> Sing!

Sing, O river!
> To the listening hills:
Thy glad music ever
> Through all nature thrills.
The lone mavis comes to sing
In the boughs that o'er thee swing,
Laden with the leaves of spring.
>> Sing, O river!
>> Sing!

Sing, O river!
   To the golden day,
Slanting sunbeams shiver,
   With thy waves at play;
Where upon thy shining brim,
Moving to thy mellow hymn,
Diamond-flashing sparkles swim.
      Sing, O river!
      Sing!

Sing, O river!
   To the silent moon,
Listening for ever
   To thy silver tune.
From their beds in the blue deep,
On thy tender face to peep,
One by one the planets creep.
      Sing, O river!
      Sing!

Sing, O river!
  To the changing year,
Flowing, flowing ever,
  Musical and clear.
Spring shall still with beauty blow,
Summer shine and autumn glow,
Winter come with cloud and snow.
    Sing, O river!
    Sing!

Sing, O river!
  Ring thy silver bells;
May thy music never
  Cease in these green dells.
In the stilly summer noon,
And at night to the sad moon,
Singing an eternal tune.
    Sing, O river!
    Sing!

## THE BRIDE.

To shady Brockenhurst she came,
    When summer days were young,
And roses lit with crimson flame,
    In conscious beauty hung.
The thrushes warbled forth her name;
    The merle her welcome sung.

The brook's low tune, the hum of bees,
    Went up from woodlands fair;
Joy whisper'd in the waving trees
    Love wander'd through the air;
Sweet voices, floating on the breeze,
    Were talking everywhere.

The dames and greybeards of the place
　　Their lady came to greet;
They lov'd her for her tender grace,
　　Her voice, so low and sweet;
And children, when they saw her face,
　　Play'd fearless at her feet.

The day-beam on the grassy slope
　　Lay, golden-bright and broad,
Symbol of love's fair horoscope
　　Sun-painted on the sod;
Broad, bright, and golden, as the hope
　　We sent in pray'r to God.

We bless'd her, and gave in her name
　　To heav'n, with heart sincere;
And,—as the rose brake into flame,
　　And songs came on the ear,—
We knew that heav'n had heard the same,
　　And made the answer clear.

# MOLLY AND I.

We sate at the farmer's festal board,
   That was spread with Christmas cheer;
With fruit we had gather'd from autumn's
      hoard;
   And the roast beef and the beer.

We caroll'd a glorious wealth of song;
   Our hearts with mirth did flow:
The wit ran loud, the ale was strong,
   And the music sweet did go.

The fiddler, he is a merry man,
    Although he may not see:
He'll sit in the blaze as long as he can,
    With his fiddle for company.

We made the fiddler stand by the wall,
    And the "Rigs of Barley" play:
We said—"strike up when you hear us call—
    One, two, and three—and away!"

The farmer,—so long dead and gone—
    Was burly then, and young:
He laugh'd as Betty was kissed by John,
    Where the mistletoe bough was hung.

And Molly and I were in our prime,
    Though now we're bent and grey:
We courted first in the sweet spring time,
    When she was the Queen of the May.

The fiddler, he kept time with his foot,
    And many a jig played he;
And Molly and I, we followed suit
    In "Sir Roger de Coverley."

There are three green hillocks in yon church-
        yard,
    We could'nt see then, I ween:
For babes have died, and times been hard,
    Now and that time between.

But Molly and I, up life's long hill,
    Through every kind of weather,
Have travell'd; and if it be God's will,
    Would end the journey together.

The Christmas time is a blessed time;
    Though another we may not see;
And the bells are ringing as sweet a chime,
    As they rang for Molly and me.

# GOD'S HILL.

Who shall into the holy place ascend,
   Or gain admittance through the golden gate,
   Where angel hands have reared in pomp and state
The temple of the universe; where bend
   In lowly reverence and love, the great
Spirits of every earth, who from the end
Of worlds remote on spreading wings have flown,
   To deck God's altar fair with purest gems,
   And crown it with their starry diadems:—

That stately temple, built of living stone,
  With glory flashing from its diamond walls;
  Where white robes gleam, and tender music falls;
And spirit-harpings mingle with the tone
  Of organ's deeper voice that from dim distance
    calls?


He only enters there whose heart is pure,
  Whose hands are white and clear from mortal
    taint,
  Whose pious love flows free from sin's restraint—
An unchcck'd river, rolling evermore;
Whose truthful words as monuments endure,
  Stately and calm, though to his hurt he swear;
Whose steadfast soul, unmov'd by passion's lure,
  Like living crystal marble shineth fair.
For him alone each overlasting door
  Swings on its golden hinge as to a king;

Seraphs bow down before him; angels sing—
"Enter, oh conqueror, to go forth no more!
For thou wast strong in battle, and hast slain
God's enemies and thine, on many a well-fought
plain."


This temple hath its image in the heart,—
　The wondrous heart of man. Angels have built
The structure stone by stone and part by part.
　Th' incarnate blood of Godhead hath been spilt
　About its deep foundations; massive, vast.
Its mighty walls, by spiritual art,
　Compact and stately in their grandeur stand,—
　Founded on solid rock, not shifting sand,—
　Immovable for ever—firm and fast.
Though suns may reel, stars sink, and worlds depart,
　It shall outlive the last great storm; the blast

That shakes the earth, and wakes the dead, and calls
The past to judgment, like a whisper falls,
Or summer's tender breath, on its eternal walls.

For it hath open'd wide its golden door
    To him, who was, and is, of glory king:
    For whom the endless heavens with praises ring;
Victor and monarch,—Lord for evermore.
And nave and transept, vestibule and tower,
    And battlemented roof, are gleaming bright
With splendours flashing from its inner shrine:
    Where the Eternal shrouds himself in light;
And sanctifies the dwelling—all divine.
There all is purity and love: the day
    Flies as on angels' wings; and hymn and psalm
For ever echo through its holy aisles;
    Life flows as flows a summer river, calm,
Where happy children sing, and bounteous nature
    smiles.

## MAGGIE BLAKE.

When sweet Maggie Blake was drown'd,
Sore we wept for her, till we
Heard the daughters of the sea
Singing from its depths profound.
Standing on the beach we heard
What they chanted,—tune and word.

Sad as music from the bell
That with death and grief doth swell,
Thus their tender cadence fell:—

"Let us weep and mourn for her,
Whom we this sad day inter
In a briny sepulchre!"

"Lightly, ah lightly lift,
Oh ye waves, her golden hair!
Loosely streaming in your drift,—
Tangled on her bosom fair."

"Float her down in ocean's arms
Westward, where the daylight dies:
Shroud, oh seaweed! Maggie's charms;
Shroud her bosom, bind her eyes."

"Fold her gentle hands to rest;
So that down the silent tide,
A dead angel she may glide:
Cross them, patient, on her breast."

"Toll, oh winds! and waters, toll!
Saddest music of the deep,
Sing a requiem for the soul
Of little Maggie!"

"Mourn and weep,
Waves that linger round her bed!
Where within a coral cave,
Yellow sands beneath her spread,
We have made her lowly grave."

"Silver shells about her lie;
Silver waters, gliding clear,
Make with your low lullaby,
Silver murmurs in her ear;
Whispering of a mother's tear,
And a grief that may not die."

## LILIES OF THE VALLEY.

What is that the thrushes cry
    Through the shaded alley?
"By the streamlet you may spy
    Lilies of the valley."

Flashing waters come and go,
    Turn, and gush, and rally:
You may hear them murmur low—
    "Lilies of the valley!"

Rose-leaves floating down the wave,
    Each a fairy's galley,
Blushing say—"Oh, pure and grave
    Lilies of the valley!"

Beetles creeping in the glade
    Make a start and sally;
Crying—"Hide us in your shade,
    Lilies of the valley!"

Honeyed buds and insects quaint
    Toy, and toss, and dally;
Singing—"Who would be a saint,
    Lilies of the valley?"

All the voices of the place
    Whisper through the alley—
"Tender is the lily's grace;
    Lilies of the valley!"

## THE BALL.

Lonely in the darkness, crouching near the wall,
List'ning to the dancers dancing at the ball,
Tripping lightly, lightly, to the music's call :—

Shivering in the night-wind, snow-flakes in her hair,
Ragged all her garments, neck and bosom bare,—
Standeth one forsaken; mute in her despair.

## THE BALL.

Ho for the carriage! hear the horses' tread!
Pamper'd pawing horses: hold them by the head!
Welcome, smiling lady, by the captain led!

Softly speaks the captain; softly speaketh he:
His voice is very tender; tender as may be:
And the lady loves to listen.  That woman! who is she?

Very brave's the captain: through the shot and shell
At deadly Balaclava, straight he rode and well:
Many a bearded Russian 'neath his sabre fell.

Brave man is the captain, for all his courtly guise;
High his look and haughty; very proud his eyes;
Yet starts he at the stranger with terrible surprise.

Blocking up the doorway, darkening the hall,
Standing like a statue, resolute and tall,
Listening to the dancers dancing at the ball;—


Standing like a statue, with stony heart and eyes,
Gazing at the captain, till his color flies,
Till his heart is shrivell'd, and his blood is ice.


"Come to me, oh captain! surely thou art mine!
See this ring, oh lady! is it not the sign
Of what he may not give thee; that never shall be
    thine?"


"Dost thou hear, oh lady? Coward! lift her head.
Her lips with blood are dabbled; with it thy hands
    are red:
Bring water: she hath fainted: God help her! she
    is dead!"

Long the years and many since that mournful day:
Buried is the lady: her tomb is worn and grey.
A sad man is the captain—he lives to weep and pray.


Dead the lonely woman, whose memory we recall,
Who stood that night, a stranger, crouching near the wall,
Listening to the dancers dancing at the ball.

# THE GIFT OF FLOWERS.

Thanks, lady, for the graceful gift,
Pluck'd from the living diadems
Of blue-eyed summer: floral gems,
To light a home where care and thrift
Are gladden'd with the sight of flowers.

Forms fair and slender, fragrant bloom,
Golden and glorious, flush the room
With beauty, whispering of green bowers,

Where roses blow, and die, and fall
To music breathing through the vale;
And linnet, thrush, and nightingale,
For ever to each other call,
Singing loud, and sweet, and clear :—


Whispering how soft winds are playing
Where its green roof the forest heaves,
And veils of beauty ivy weaves
Round trunks with hoary time decaying :—


Whispering of the noise of leaves,
And the swinging and the swaying,
And the pleasant things they're saying,
To the young birds of the year,
Who with drows'd eye and list'ning ear,
Out of their downy dwellings peer.

Whispering of the beams that quiver
On the diamond-dimpled river,
Ever through the woodlands straying;
Where tender-verdured boughs have made
Cathedral-window traceries,
And leafy lanes, and canopies,
Fleck'd with shimmering shine and shade:—

Whispering low of silent dells,
Green with moss and feathery plume
Of fern, and gilt with furzy bloom,
And bright with purply-crimson bells
Of foxglove; in whose marbled cells
Many a quaint and mystic line
Lies written by a pen divine;
Where flaunting zephyrs gaily sweep,
And load the passing wind with balm
Of meadows, lying in the calm
Grand sunshine, lazily asleep:—

Whispering of ancestral trees,
    And cry of mavis, merle, and rook,
    From every wooded, leafy nook,
Swelling and dying with the breeze:—


Whispering more than all the story
    Of the Father's love and care,
    Who made all things good and fair,
And crown'd the great earth with His glory,


Thanks, O lady, for the flow'rs,
    And the fancies they have brought;
    Soothing to the troubled thought:
Balm and peace for weary hours.

# THE STREET AND THE RIVER.

I stand at my warehouse window,
   And look down the busy street:
I hear the talk of the traders;
   The tramp of their eager feet.

I hear the chatter of children,
   Threading their way to the schools;
They are deep in "Lindley Murray,
Pence-table, Spelling, and Rules."

## THE STREET AND THE RIVER.

A marriage peal is ringing:
   How the big bells clash and roll!
But the loudest bell in the belfry,
   Ere night, for a death may toll.

Hoarse comes the noise of labour,
   Sturdy, and full, and strong;
And sweet from that open casement,
   The voice of a lady's song.

To work, church, pleasure, or market,
   The thronging people go;
Like streams, twisted hither and thither,
   That in green meadows flow.

A lord rides forth on his charger;
   Here is a child in tears;
A butcher-lad with a basket;
   A net on his pony's ears.

## THE STREET AND THE RIVER.

A beggar in rags and tatters,
   A lady in velvet and silk,
A painter, a noted author,
   A sweep, the man with the milk.

A maiden with golden tresses;
   A priest, a soldier, a fop;
A man crying "water-cresses!"
   An urchin spinning a top.

A missionary, a miser,
   A tradesman wrinkled with care,
Two rogues, a dozen policemen;
   These on their way to the mayor.

Trade, physic, law, and gospel;
   Music, and mammon, and mirth;
All that a man may care for,
   Between his death and his birth.

## THE STREET AND THE RIVER.

And green hills skirting the river,—
   A shade from the glare and the heat;
And the musical waters for ever
   That murmur and glide at their feet.

A beautiful shadowy vision,
   A tender prophetical shore,
Of woods, hills, and waters Elysian,
   When the work of the world shall be o'er.

## THE FANCY BALL.

(NEWLANDS.)

Bright is the scene: and sweetly falls
   The fairy music on the ear,
   As sparkling water singing clear
To its grey rocks or woody walls.

Bright is the scene: the lamps are lit:
   Away with thoughts of grief and gloom,
   Where, graceful, down the gilded room,
Youth, manhood, glory, beauty flit.

Bright is the scene: the moments fly
    On wings of gladness through the soul:
    Life's wheels on golden axles roll:
Joy lifts his magic cup on high.

Yet here, amid the sparkling throng,
    The solemn-storied past is seen:
    Prince, priest, and cardinal, and queen,
And knight, and noble, known to song.

Here sweeps Pescara's queenly dame;
    Fair daughter of a mighty race;
    The first in honor as in place;
The glory of Colonna's name.

And floating graceful through the dance,
    Comes sweet Lamballe, with Scotland's queen,
    And tender, glorious Anne Boleyn,
With fair Elizabeth of France.

Here's princely Buckingham : and here
   Rowena, hapless maid, doth move;
   And here's Du Barry, queen of love;
And Raleigh, stately and severe.

And many a kirtled dame that graced
   Revel, and masque, and courtly ball,
   In royal Tudor's palace hall,—
Frill'd, pointed, jewell'd and belaced.

Knight, baron, love-lorn cavalier,
   Earl, courtier, page, and warrior bravo;
   Grey councillor, sedate and grave;
Statesman, and ruler,—all are here.

Stars of a grand historic time :
   Stars of a time that long hath set;
   Their very names are mighty yet;
Gems of a nation's golden prime.

In this fair scene not of place ;
For it is fitting they should cast
Their glory's shadow, dim and vast,
Where beauty moves, and love, and grace.

Press to the dance : the moments fly
On wings of gladness through the soul :
Life's wheels on golden axles roll :
Joy lifts his magic cup on high.

## THE WAVE.

A wave came singing through Milford Reach,
    A wreath of pearls in his lordly hand:
A maiden was weeping on the beach:
He came to her feet; his soothing speech
    Said—"Fly with me, lady, from the land."

"Listen, oh lady mine!"—he said,—
    Said and sang with his silver tongue:—
"Life is weary when love is dead,
And hope hath gone, and joy hath fled,
    And friendship's knell hath long been rung."

"Desolate maid! no longer weep:
　Say but a prayer, and come to me:
Quiet dwells in the soundless deep,
Sorrowful hearts are hushed to sleep,
　And tears are unknown beneath the sea."

The maid, she listen'd all too long:
　The wave came over the shining sand:
He won her with his wondrous song;
She leapt to his arms so wide and strong;
　And swift he bore her from the land.

## THE OLD CHURCH ORGAN.

"Mourn not, oh wanderer from afar!"—thus sang
The old church organ, while the player swept
His fingers softly o'er the chords, and kept
Time to all tender cadences that hung,
And fell in drops of melody, and wept
In music, and through all the building crept
In waves that rippling murmured a low rhyme,
Soothing and sad. Then memories that had slept,

Awoke and cried aloud: a buried time
Came back all bright and rosy with the prime
Of life in its gay beauty: boyhood leapt
Forth from the misty years: youth's golden clime
Return'd with peal of organ and the chime
Of Sunday bells: a fair land where I stept
With lightsome foot through many a treasur'd scene,
Untroubled as if grief had never been.


And in the pulpit, thundering forth the law,
The hoary parson, buried deep for years;
The beadle stern, who pull'd my wicked ears;
The clerk, who did with such a rook-like caw,
From a lean throat his quavering "Amens" draw;
Pew-opener, sexton, verger frowning fierce;
And some that I had mourn'd with many tears;
Some, ah, how many! these in mind I saw:
My father, and my mother at his side;

And next to her my brother, with his bride,

In modest Sunday robes : a face more sweet

God made not.   I remember how she cried.

Her pretty chin I tickled with a straw

For dozing in the sermon.   Ah, she died!

She and my brother lie at father's feet :

Their tomb is near the porchway, just outside.


The schoolboys gathered here, a noisy throng,

Rude as the sea waves, ardent, never still :

There stood the imperious master, strong of will,

Muttering old scraps of Greek or Roman song :

And near him the meek usher, limp and long,

Who wept melodious sorrows through his flute.

The ruddy rogues pass'd sweetmeats round, and
    fruit ;

Played " toss the kerchief," made the missile fly

Birdlike, from hand to hand ; some slyly read

The tale unfinished in that morning's bed;
One, worse than others, brought a stock of pins,
And prick'd his neighbours as they mourn'd their sins;
And heard, delighted, heavenwards-turn'd his eye,
The sighing of his victims, as they bled:
He pinn'd—the cane fell with explosive crack,—
The master and the usher back to back.


I mark'd the hatchments blazon'd on the wall;
The epitaphs and kneeling effigies;
The solemn lies about the dead, to please
The living; dusty, tatter'd flags that fall
Piecemeal; the carvéd monumental frieze;
Urns; skull and cross bones; heraldry that blazed
In fields of deadly strife, or festal hall
Of chivalry; the knightly helmets grazed
By sweep of sword in battle's bloody fray;

And storied altars tipt with marble flames,
Recording benefactions made to cheat
The conscience on a sinner's dying day :—
I saw them slowly mouldering, as is meet,
With nobles', and churchwardens' meaner names.


These built the gallery, for which they laid
The public under contribution : this
Provided chandeliers, for which he paid :
A noble act; his soul is now in bliss.
These had the organ mended; and 'tis said
Were large subscribers—**J. Green** and **Will. Drew.**
Behold their sainted names with gold thick laid
On every letter. Both were well to do.
This was Drew's seat; Green had the corner pew.
And here's a cherub painted in black strokes ;
And underneath another name—**John Nokes.**

John Nokes is with the cherubim, be sure:
He gave the great lock for the western door,
And two keys: one was lost: he gave one more.


And through the eastern traceried window came
The shining of the morning sun; it fell
In flashing drops of crystal crimson flame
Upon the altar-cloth, and o'er the name
Of Him who for us conquer'd death and hell.
It made around the preacher's silver hair
A mystic halo; threw a sanguine stain
That splash'd and rippled o'er the Book of Prayer,
And sparkled in red cascades down the wall;
It glimmer'd in the roof; the columns tall
Caught the live splendour: still it grew and spread.
On oaken pews it threw a ruddy glare;
It touch'd with fire the legends of the dead,
And with its glory filled the chancel fair;

Floor, galleries, pillars, bathed in golden rain,
And martyrs burning on the storied pane.

Again the organ brake into a roll
And crash of melody—a mighty peal
Of gladness; then most soothingly did steal
A softer strain that wander'd through my soul,
And touch'd all tender memories of the leal
And lov'd, that I had lost and wept; whose names
Were writ on the great tombstone near the door;
Names, naught but names, of those who nevermore
Shall raise the sacred song, or pious kneel
In prayer: cut down by death's remorseless steel;
Lover, and friend, and parents; little frames
Of children, fairest buds that deathless bloom
In Eden's realm; and one sweet maid; ah! slowly
We'll speak of her: all music, all perfume
Her life; her soul as lilies, white and lowly:
Her death one summer's eve,—as calm and holy.

We called her "Ella," and we lov'd the name:
There was a wealth of music in the word;
And music came to her, as to the bird
That sings when day hath quench'd his golden flame.
All love, all tenderness, all goodness came
Into her heart, as sunshine on the sea:
All lov'd her, she lov'd all; and she lov'd me,
And was my life's sole glory, joy, and crown.
Ah, God of mine! that such a change should be!
That death with his rude foot should trample down
Hopes that did make a heav'n of earth; and drag
Life trailing at his gloomy wheels!  She fell
In beauty, as the roses fall, when storms
Darken the summer heavens.  For her the bell
Heavily tolled, as if it fain would lag
On duty, as she went to earth's cold arms.

I left the church, and went out in the air,
Where I might look up to the quiet sky,

And let its great calm soothe my misery.

My grief was heavy, more than I could bear:
It fell with such a pitiless weight; it crush'd
Out of my soul the long-pent tears, that rush'd
In sudden rivers that could not be stayed.
There was the linnet singing by her grave,
Where through the summer day the lindens wave:
The roses, planted where my heart is laid,
Bore a few blossoms: zephyrs lightly played
With lilies of the valley; insects made
A low melodious thrumming; birds and bees
Disported, now in sunshine, now in shade;
And "Ella! Ella! Ella!"—sang the breeze.

## MY LADY'S PLACE.

Oh would I were the rose that clings
   About my lady's lattice pane!
Oh would I were the bird that sings
   To cheer her fancy with its strain!

Or those twin-lilies tall, that grace
   The porchway; or the vine that weaves
A veil of beauty round the place,
   In graceful, labyrinthine leaves.

Or the great willow tree, that shades
    Her pathway where the waters run,
And from the saintliest of maids
    Checks the bold glances of the sun.

Or yonder swan that charms the eye,
    A distant vision, dimly seen,
On crystal waters gliding by:
    My lady loves him well, I ween.

Or that soft wind of dying bliss,
    Fainting with incense of the south,
That takes its last expiring kiss
    Of sweetness from her rosy mouth.

Or the frail, broken flow'r that lies
    Breathing last odours at her foot;
For one kind look from such dear eyes,
    Ah me, such dying were too sweet!

So I might linger in the place,
>By lake, and lawn, and river fair;
And win, perchance, my lady's grace,
And dwell for ever with her there.

## LONG AGO!

In the days of long ago,
Summer skies were all aglow
With a crystal golden flame:
How the glory went and came,
As it cometh nevermore!
Then the vaulted shining blue,
Curtain'd heaven from my view:
Then the angel forms that keep
Watch by God's great temple
    door,
Through the veil would some-
    times peep:

Then the sun that flush'd the west
With his majesty and state,
Open'd to my soul the gate
Of the city of the blest.

In those days of long ago,
Silver-shining rivers ran
With a purer, brighter flow,
With a sweeter music than
Falleth now upon my ear.
Through the joyful woods they went
With a burst of merriment;
Singing to the laughing year,
Singing to the summer birds,
Who the summons answer'd clear.
Then my spirit's inner sense
Knew the mystery of words
Thus in nature's language given;

And the earth to me was heaven
In those days of innocence;
In those days of long ago.

In those days of long ago,
Days, ah nevermore to be!
Life was all a raree-show,
Fair and beautiful to me.
Friendship's beacon bright and
    true
Threw its light along the way;
Time in radiant circles flew;
Love and gladness, mirth and
    play,
Held unbroken holiday.

Now the tender dream is dead;
Hope hath vanish'd; joy hath
    fled;

At the gate of happy years
Grief is standing, blind with
  tears:
Lips that whispered love are still,
Faithful hearts lie cold and low,
Where the stream that skirts the
  hill,
Mourns the days of long ago.

## THE LAST MINSTREL.

The wind was roaring on the sea; the snow fell
    thick and fast:
The forest leaves, like frightened birds, were flying
    on the blast:
Dark clouds had gather'd in the sky: the light was
    blurred and dim:
The poplars by the garden walk look'd desolate
    and grim:

The swollen river sobbing ran along the dreary lane;
When Robin Redbreast came a tapping at the window pane.

"Oh Robin, darling Robin! oh Robin, ever dear!
The snow beats on your scarlet breast; oh wherefore come you here?
Cold falls the night; the wind is high; the flow'rs are dead you know:
Your nest fell from its place last night; 'tis on the ground below:
No leaves are on the bushes now; the frost has taken all:
Seek shelter, pretty Robin, in the ivy on the wall."

"Oh ladies, pretty ladies, sure Robin's heart is sad:
From morn to night, from night to morn, there's nothing to be had:

The cruel, cruel winter's come his dearest hopes
to kill :
There is no worm above the ground, nor berry on
the hill :
His little ones are all grown up, thank God! one
trouble less :
They're gone to get their living now ; but how, he
cannot guess."

"The fir-tree by the garden gate is laden thick with
snow :
Within its shelter'd hiding place I hear the tempests
blow ;
Its branches whisper as they wave, and where their
shadows spread,
I sit, as in a tomb, and muse of faded things and
dead :
Yet sometimes will my heart awake ; my soul with
love will thrill ;

And I come to sing my little tune upon your
    window-sill."


"I make no quarrel with my lot: the summer days.
    were long;
Its skies were very clear and bright; the world was
    filled with song:
My nest lay bosom'd in green leaves; the scent of
    many flowers
Rose from earth's thousand altars fair; sweet ran
    the sunny hours:
My heart was glad—all things were glad,—in the
    year's golden prime;
'Tis right a change should come about; and this
    is winter time."


"The swallow may not skim the lake, nor circle
    through the sky;

Gone is the tuneful nightingale, and hush'd the
    cushat's cry;
The blackbird and the thrush are mute; the linnet
    sings no more;
The goldfinch sits with drooping wing by the black
    river shore;
Dead, dark, and dumb, the world hath grown,—
    brown, desolate, and sere;
And I, the last of minstrels, sing the death-song
    of the year."

"I could not let him die unsung; nor see his hoary
    hairs
Sink, all unmourn'd, into the grave; though I
    have heavy cares;
I may not sing another spring: again the flow'r
    and tree
May come with pleasant shade and scent for you,
    but not for me.

My heart with love and grief must break: woe's
  me! woe's me!—I cry:
A crumb or two is all I ask, dear souls, before I
  die."


"Oh Robin, darling Robin, oh Robin ever dear!
Come, pretty minstrel, to our hearts; we'll give
  you Christmas cheer.
Along the window-sill for you with loving hands
  we'll spread
Each night and morn, and all day long, our crumbs
  of cake and bread;
And should you fear the schoolboys rude, when
  gathering on the slide,
We'll put the window-frame ajar, and you shall
  come inside."


"So Robin, pretty Robin, sweet Robin ever dear!

You shall not break your little heart, nor die with
    this old year:
But you shall sing through many a spring; and
    summer buds shall peep
Again into your cosy nest; and summer winds
    shall sweep
About your pleasant dwelling place: so weep not,
    Robin dear!
Though you, the last of minstrels, sing the death-
    song of the year.

# EVERMORE.

By Milford's lonely shore
   A stately lady sits:
She listens to the roar
Of waves that evermore
Roam ocean's heaving floor:
   A golden shadow flits
On the billows, as they meet
The sands beneath her feet,
Where the waters break and beat
   Evermore;
Break and beat
   Evermore!
   Ever, evermore!

## EVERMORE.

She traces on the sands
   A name, that bids her weep;
Anon she wrings her hands,
As the liquid foaming bands
Sweep the writing from the lands
   To the cruel, cruel deep.

And 'mid the watery roar,
She hears in thought a bell,
Tolling a ceaseless knell
For one she loveth well
   Evermore!
Loveth well
   Evermore!
   Ever, evermore!


Lo! on the western sky
   Lies a purple, painted shore:
Temple and tow'r have met

With mosque and minaret,
And walls of golden fret,
  With glory sprinkled o'er.
Oh lady, lift thine eye!
She sees; but weepeth yet:
Shall her faithful heart forget
A fairer day that's set,
  Gone down for evermore?
  Evermore!
Sunk for evermore!
  Ever, evermore!

# SUNDAY MORNING.

The day is calm, and cold, and clear:
    I wander, thoughtful, through the town,
    'Mid houses, silent, square, and brown;
And mark where the old church doth rear

Its hoary walls and reverend head
    O'er its tall neighbours in the street;
    While, in the belfry, low and sweet,
The chimes seem talking of the dead:

Now from the chancel window bars
    A solemn sound begins to roll :
    The organ, lifting up its soul,
Doth sing, as sang the morning stars.

And now the mighty quire of bells
    Swings out its music on the air ;
    And from their homes, in garments fair,
The people come, as from their cells

Came forth the monks of olden days,
    When broider'd cope and blazon'd cross,
    White alb, and mitre's silken gloss,
Pass'd slowly down these ancient ways.

The day is cold, and calm, and clear ;
    The wind is low, the sea is still ;
    The river, underneath the hill,
Flows soberly in quiet cheer.

The ships, moored to their silent quay,
>   Move idly on the creeping tides;
>   And foam-bells break along their sides,
Down the smooth pathway to the sea.


They float, these foam-bells, as in years
>   And centuries that have gone before;
>   As they must float for evermore,—
These silver-whirling shining spheres.


So floated they in history's prime,
>   When Britons, on these rushy banks,
>   Battled with Cæsar's serried ranks,—
The patriots of that olden time.


Or when in later days the Dane
>   Swept fiercely up the broad lagoon;
>   And grim and stark beneath the moon,
Lay Celt and Teuton, gash'd and slain.

The day is cold, and calm, and clear;
    Calm are the woods—divinely calm:
    The trees are priests; each lifts a palm
Bared, Godwards. Underneath, the sere

Dropp'd leaves are lying; they are naught:
    They were the glories of their time;
    They had their tender birth and prime,
And died: but to th' immortal thought,

They speak as nature ever speaks,
    Through the pure soul's sublimer sense,
    To him that pays her reverence,
And of her wisdom, wisdom seeks.

Through tangled briar glides the snake;
    The fox sleeps lonely in his den;
    The rabbit burrows in the glen;
The deer lies couchant in the brake.

The blue kingfisher woos the stream,
> A painted hermit of the shades;
> But, startled, flies to deeper glades;
And with him flies my wayward dream.


Old woods, with God's own beauty crown'd!
> Town, church, and river wandering by!
> What is the link, the sympathy,
By which to you my soul is bound?


I cannot tell; but can descry,
> That, for the better or the worse,
> The patterns of the universe
Must in that soul for ever lie.


Form, light, and sunshine; shade, and tint
> Painted on earth, and sky, and sea,
> (Divinest writing) are to me
Symbol, or spiritual hint

Of somewhat to be understood,
 Of higher wisdom, wider scope
 Of love, and charity, and hope,
And faithful working into good.

## NIGHT.

How dark the tree-tops loom across the skies;
  Splendour hath left the gardens gay and proud:
  The earth lies black and silent as a cloud:
Sound, there is none; save when the cricket cries
  From turf or mossy twig.  My heart is bowed,
My soul is melted into eye and ear.
  This is God's funeral methinks.  Her shroud
The reverent night doth lay along His bier.
  The heavens are all alive with golden eyes
Of angels gazing downwards with a tear
  Of sympathy and pity; it may be
Of gladness that the end is drawing near,
  When God shall rise again, and evil flee,
And doubt lie solv'd, and mystery grow clear.

## THE SLEEPLESS NIGHT.

"I could not sleep in the night, Mary!
  Nor till the dawn of the day:
The children were in the place, Mary!
  I heard them talk and play."

"Oh, what is that you say, uncle?
  The night was still and calm,
Save rosebuds touching the window-pane,
  And the nightingale in psalm."

"You heard the song in the garden,
   And the rosebuds came with a tap
At the door of the wonderful palace,
   That fancy builds in a nap."

"I heard the rose at the window,
   And the night-bird singing clear:
But sweeter voices than his, Mary!
   Were sounding in my ear."

"Fair is the rose at the window,
   In leaf, in bud, in bloom;
But fairer than light the forms last night,
   That came into my room."

"I kiss'd their shining faces,
   I stroked each golden head;
Children three come back to me,
   Out of the land of the dead."

"'This,'—they said—'is our father,
Who wept when we went away;
He will soon be laid in the Liten,
For he is old and grey.'"

"A holy song they sung, Mary!
Of loving words to me:
Each tender strain had a sweet refrain,—
'Father, we wait for thee.'"

"Open the window wide, Mary;
Lift up this grey old head:
Do you hear them calling to me, Mary?
I COME!" Th' old man was dead.

## THE COMING OF THE KING.

---

A trumpet rang within my heart:
    The King stood at His temple door:
    I fain had closed it evermore,
And kept it from His sway apart.

Its walls wore down; its courts defiled;
    Weeds, ruins, reptiles, fill'd the place:
    Ah me! 'twas in an evil case,
With desolation running wild.

It was not always so: a day,
    A long time—ah, how long ago!
    Had been, when like the driven snow,
Its glories met the morning ray.

'Twas joy to count its stately tow'rs:
    Its massive bulwarks as they stood
    Immoveable to ev'ry rude
Assault and shock of evil pow'rs.

Then joy and splendour dwelt within,
    And strains of sweetest music rose
    At break of day and ev'ning's close,
To heav'nly melodies akin.

But ah! the weak castellan slept,
    Oblivious to the warder's call;
    While foemen undermined the wall,
And through the breach to vict'ry swept.

They chained me down in deepest cells:
    My brow was branded with their mark;
    Until I learn'd to love the dark,
To love my very manacles.

They cast me loose; they bade me sing
    The songs that I had lov'd before:
    But music came to me no more;
For I was traitor to the King.

And when they left me to my woe,
    With jibe and jest they pass'd away:
    Their dreadful work was done, to lay
The temple of my love so low.

And so from day to day I went
    The stately ruins round about:
    My spirit dazed with fear and doubt,
Repented it could not repent.

He came! his mighty trumpet rang
    Through all the portals of my soul,
    Like waves of thunder when they roll
O'er sea and sky with brazen clang.

Ten thousand thousand legions bore
    His regal banners flaming high:
    Their pennons rippled on the sky:
Their shields his red cross emblem wore.

I drew the bolts, undrawn for years;
    I saw him, heard him, felt him come;
    He spake; I spoke not; I was dumb:
I only answer'd him with tears.

My head was hidden in his breast:
    My shame was fain his glance to shun:
    He raised me, kiss'd me, call'd me
        "Son!"
Said he had come to be my guest:

To build again the broken walls;
    Once more to raise the fallen towers;
    To fill with sunshine, music, flowers,
The ruin'd and dismantled halls.

He bade them healing water bring,
    That flows in Eden, pure and sweet;
    They cleans'd my stains from head to
        feet;
They brought me, robed, before the King.

Then did their heav'nly strength uprear
    The temple, stately built, and strong;
    And borne on breath of harps, a song
Was heard—most musical and clear:—

"Lift up thine head, eternal gate!
    Unfold, thou everlasting door!
    And enter, to go forth no more,
Oh King, with all thy train and state!"

A beam, a flash of golden fire,
　　Along the battlements did run;
　　A glory brighter than the sun
Flush'd wall and window, roof and spire.

And though the opening portals came
　　A holy psalm that rose and fell,
　　In waves that carried on their swell
The music of some mighty name.

"Lift up thine head, eternal gate!
　　Unfold, thou everlasting door!
　　And enter, to go forth no more,
Oh King, with all thy train and state!"

He came with cymbals sounding high,
　　With harp, and viol, and the clang
　　And clash of clarion tones that rang
Along the farthest depths of sky.

The sea of music rose, and dash'd
    Its waves through all the sacred pile;
    White robes gleam'd down each
        column'd aisle;
Gems of immortal glory flash'd.

So pass'd he to his temple throne:
    Harps, crowns, and sceptres lined
        his way:—
    I heard the minstrels sing and say—
"Lord, take the kingdom, 'tis thine own!"

"Who is this King of joy, on whom
    These solemn services await?
    Such awful dignity and state,
Who may--who dares--such pomp assume?"

"It is the Lord, in battle strong,
    For whom this mighty rapture flows;
    Monarch and victor o'er his foes;
And his this everlasting song."

His guards, in radiant order set,
 Keep watch and ward by wall and door;
 For foes must enter nevermore,
Where love like his and mine hath met.

Days pass: the rapid seasons fly:
 The years their ceaseless round renew:
 Love is than time more strong and true:
Nor his, nor mine, shall ever die.

Thine is the kingdom: thine the crown!
 My God, my Father, I am thine;
 And by the heavenly compact, mine
Art thou, thy glory and renown.

I bring thee nothing: I am worse
 Than nothing: I am naught but sin:
 Yet, by thy grace, am close akin
To him who rules the universe.

## HURST CASTLE.

Old castle, that dost lift thy rugged front,
Wrinkled with storms, and dinted by the sea's
Perpetual stroke : old greybeard! wind and breeze
Break and sweep moaning round thy walls; the
    brunt
Of tempest still is on thee : thou dost hear
Th' Almighty's mightiest fingers press the keys
Of ocean, till through all the liquid sphere,
Music with thunder runs, and rings, and leaps
From wave to rocky shore, to cliff and sky,

Shaking the world: the white-wing'd seagulls fly
Screaming round thy grey battlements; the deeps
Flow weltering to thy feet: the billow sweeps
Thee with his watery shot: the driving gale
Batters thee with salt spray, rude rain, and volley'd hail.


Where are those grim old warriors, who kept
With brand and bow, with shield and helm and spear,
Thy watch and ward through every ancient year,
When English Harry reign'd, and Wolsey wept?
Or when in later days th' Armada swept
To its own woe along that western shore;
Or that stern time when Cromwell's awful name
Rose redden'd, lurid with red Naseby's fame;
And to thy lonely dungeon by the wave,
A royal captive—soon a martyr—came;

Or, later still, when in thy shade a grave,
Rome's hapless minion found, who perished here:
Where are they—bowman, swordsman, musketeer?
What answer make the waters? — "Gone for
    evermore!"


Gone! floating down the flowing tides of time;
Life's battle fought—its labour done; they rest
Well; lifted on th' eternal sea, whose breast
Still bears them onward: winds and waters chime
Their lullaby: in everlasting rhyme
The billows sing about them in the caves,
And chant their story to the silent rocks;
Their deeds, words, fancies, day of death, their
    graves;
Their faith—Pelagian, Arian, orthodox;
Their songs, if they did sing; prayers, if they
    prayed;

Who wept when they were buried; what was said
Or sung of them by others; age and date;
Costume and mode of thought; life, manners,
    fate :—
All this and more, of each old sentinel,
Unto his listening shores the wild sea loves to tell.


But not for thee, old castle, is there rest :
More fierce, and grim, and stately, than of old;
Thy features fashioned in a sterner mould;
Rude welcome proff'rest thou to warlike guest,
Thou warder of the waters! Thou would'st play
A dreadful game along the crested waves,
Laughing hoarse thunder as into their graves
Thou sendest fleets, ships, captains, crews,—thy
    prey;
Should such essay thy terrors, madly bold.
Smile yet, oh stronghold! See! the tempests fly:

Eastwards they move; their cloudy wings unfold;
And there is peace in heaven. How clear the sky!
The day's red god flames down the golden west,
And golden ripples burn on ocean's heaving breast.

## FRANKY BROWN.

Franky Brown is dead and gone,
    Crippled, silly, old, and poor:
Death has taken him in pawn,
    Closed accounts, and shut the door.

Franky Brown was half a fool;
    Stunted body; crooked limb;
Head of lead, and brain of wool:
    Many a laugh we had at him.

We no more shall hear him talk
    Words from foolish fancies spun;
Through the town no more he'll walk;
    His old crutch's work is done.

Knell, for poor old Franky toll!
    Parson, read the words of grace!
God hath loos'd the pauper's soul:
    Death hath dignified his face.

Gone, where fortune's haughty claim
    Is not recognised, nor made;
Where, of wisest worldling's fame,
    There is nothing sung or said.

He, for well nigh fourscore years,
    (Threescore years and ten and seven)
Lived among us, who now clears
    His dazed sight, we trust, in heaven.

Care of living, griefs of age,
    Franky knew not: God is just;
Who made simpleton and sage,
    And who brings them back to dust.

His poor life a problem was,
    Dark, and manifold, and vast;
Yet it will to him and us
    Be made plain and clear at last.

Place him in his lowly grave;
    Churchyard mould upon his breast:
Lay him with the fair and brave;
    He will not their sleep molest.

Lay him low, and let him be;
    Leave him to the Father's grace:
Many a better man than he
    Hath not such a resting place.

## THE SPECTRES OF BUCKLAND RINGS.

In lonely Buckland Rings, a lamp
    At night will slowly glide;
And some have heard a soldier's tramp,
And seen him, in the mist and damp,
Go round the solitary camp;
    A woman at his side.

A shield of Rome the spectre bears;
    His helmet hath a gleam
Of silver; and the sword he wears
Makes awful glittering: he stares
As one, who, startled unawares,
    Wakes from a troubled dream.

She holds a dagger in her grasp,
    It hath a golden hilt:
She holds it in a ruthless clasp,
Yet, as she gazes, seems to gasp
With horror, for the blood from hasp
    To point runs, newly spilt.

Her left hand bears the lamp, that flings
    A pale, uncertain ray
Across the melancholy Rings,
To where the shallow brooklet sings;
And strangest shrieks and murmurings
    Are heard along their way.

Down to the little brook they go,
    The brook that skirts the hill;
Then cry they forth a cry of woe,
Most sad, most terrible; when lo!
Their forms like fire a moment glow,
    Vanish, and all is still.

'Tis said there runs some ancient rhyme
    Of murder, calling still
For vengeance; some mysterious crime
Committed in a bygone time;
And how from vespers until prime
    These spectres haunt the hill.

I know not what the truth may be,
    But this I dare aver,—
That death is but a troubled sea
To those who die in guilt; and he
Must fly from sin, who hopes to flee
    A restless sepulchre.

## LEILA.

(A MEMORIAL.)

---

The autumn day was bright; the leaves
   Lay thick and crumpled in the road:
   The homely village garden glow'd
With fruit: the lowly cottage eaves

Were curtain'd deep with yellow vines,
   And ivy, and sweet clematis,
   Whose stars of snow the zephyrs kiss;
Where rose with jasmine intertwines,

And the canariensis blooms,
  Its golden spangles gaily flinging
  Into windows, whence the singing
Of children, pent in narrow rooms,

Floats in music pure and clear,
  Over the meadows still and green,
  Over the river that glides between,
And through the hazy atmosphere:

Floating far, and floating near:
  Like a song we loved, or strain,
  We shall never hear again;
Floating still on fancy's ear.

Our shoulders bore a grievous load,
  Draped and shrouded, cas'd in oak;
  Our hearts were smitten with a stroke
Too keen for feeling, as we strode

With measur'd step, and mournful pace,
    Bearing our Leila to her rest,
    Who lay with meek hands on her breast
Cross'd, as when last she prayed for grace;

But with closed eyes and deep'ning shades
    Upon her face, of ashen gray;
    Too deep—too gray—to fade away,
Till death, that fadeth all things, fades.

Full heavy was the load that press'd,
    Dead, leaden, dull, upon our strength;
    Our souls were heavier: at length
We reach'd a chapel, looking west,

Facing the death-bed of the sun;
    The sea a mile away, a belt
    Of glory, into which did melt
The passing vessels, one by one.

It was a quiet place of rest,
  From worldly care and noise shut out;
  Where scarce is heard the boatman's
    shout,
From the far river's brimming breast.

We heard the swallow piping by,
  The linnet singing in the trees,
  The leaves that chatter'd to the breeze,
That sang its tenderest melody.

These alone broke the silence deep
  That broods for ever in the shade,
  Where we our loving Leila laid,
And turned aside, unseen to weep.

"Dust unto dust"—the parson cried—
  "All flowers must fade—and pass away!"
  What has not faded—since the day
When gentle Leila died?

## "FIDDLERS' RACE."

A fiddler blind, whose name was Joyce,
    Once liv'd in Lymington;
And proud was he of his six boys,
    Rare fiddlers every one.

His sons grew up a lusty band,
    None less than six feet high :
Each, with his fiddle in his hand,
    Could fiddle famously.

The Joyces' fiddling, far and wide,
  Was famed the country through;
And scarce a wedding knot was tied,
  But the feast they went unto.

One day to John a message came
  Across the Solent Sea,
That all must hie to Whippinghame,
  Where a bridal feast would be.

John's wife a bitter temper had,
  She had a nagging tongue,
She nagg'd at husband, friend, and lad:
  John sometimes wished her hung.

Quoth goody Joyce,—" You shall no more
  At weddings be allowed!"
" I'll go,"—said John—" if to this door
  I come back in a shroud!"

"Aye, come back so!"—she cried,—"and
    then
No further boon I'll crave,
But when you're buried, worst of men!
    To dance upon your grave."

Then all the fiddlers cross'd the sea,
    And to the wedding came;
And through the night right merrily
    They played at Whippinghame.

Though John's old eyes were blind and dark,
    Yet would you deftly swear
He was the gayest, blithest spark
    Of all that sparkled there.

But when the morning broke, the sky
    Was black with storm and cloud;
The sea rose, and the wind was high;
    The whirlpool roar'd aloud.

John's boat was for a moment seen,
   Sore labouring in the waves;
Then lost: the whirlpool made, I ween,
   That morning seven graves.

When goody Joyce lay down that night,
   And thought upon her deeds,
John's ghost came in, a shocking sight!
   All dripping, hung with weeds.

"Oh, goody Joyce, I and your boys
   No more will be allowed
With merry hearts to play our parts:
   We're dead!—behold my shroud!"

"Now learn your doom: each night to come,
   A ghost, along the wave;
From twelve o'clock till the crow of the cock,
   To dance upon my grave!"

At morn the goody called a priest,
And all her sins confess'd,
And died; but could not be released:
Her soul will never rest.

That whirlpool is a name of fear;
The sailor shuns the place:
Her ghost at midnight wanders near:
Men call it—"Fiddlers' Race!"

# THE GROANING TREE OF BADDESLEY.

When Parson Warner wrote for fame,
   (A learned antiquarian he,)
A wonder to each village dame
   Was found in Baddesley's groaning tree.

It grew as any other elm,
   Tall, fair, and vigorous, as might be :
In all King George's island realm
   A statelier trunk you could not see.

Alack! it groaned by night and day,
   Like some poor soul in torments dire;
Till half the village ran away,
   And half were ready to expire.

The world came: fashion, fancy, trade:
   The weird phenomenon to mark:
The people listen'd, shudder'd, pray'd:
   "Horror! it groans again! oh hark!"

From Pylewell Palace, England's king
   A visit to the marvel paid:
The court cried—"Sire! a wondrous thing!"
   "Strange tree! strange tree!" the monarch said.

Some swore the noise came from the roots:
   The tree perchance had gouty toes,
Enclosed in a tight pair of boots;
   And thus the dreadful sound arose.

Some said 'twas water; dropsical
    Disease, occasion'd by much rain;
Some, wind, that inward troubling shall
    Put trees, as well as men, in pain.


The priest his great chin wagg'd, and said
    "There is some mystery, no doubt!"
Then scratch'd for something in his head—
    "The puzzle is to find it out."


A wise philosopher came next,
    And reason'd much of nature's laws,
The rule of causes and effects:
    The difficulty was—the cause.


In vain: the wisest heads were done:
    Disputes grow high, and words uncivil:
All shook with fear who came for fun:
    'Twas something, very strange and evil.

Then in the trunk they bored a hole:
This stopped the groaning evermore:
For through the rift th' imprisoned soul
Flew out; it could not stand a bore.

At length, uprooted in the mead
It lay; such fate was just and fit:
Naught else was known; but all agreed
The "old one" must have been in it.

## THE SEVEN BROTHERS.

Hear'st thou the brothers that dwell altogether,
    Singing—" one, two, three, four, five, six, and
        seven ; "
Whose tower is hoary with time and the weather,
    Wrinkled and worn with the tempests of heaven ?
Over whose gray walls, steadily creeping,
    Crawleth the ivy on timorous feet ;
From whose tall battlements silently sweeping,
    The bat and the owl pass over the street.

Resting their heads on the mildew'd church rafters;
  Whispering, murmuring, brother to brother;
Low-tinkled melodies, musical laughters,
  Rising and passing from one to the other.
Tidings of township and parish they gather;
  Who has been buried, or christen'd, or wed;
How the bride for her lover left mother and
      father;
  News of the living, and news of the dead.


Grey-bearded gossips, quaint memories keeping,
  Of those in whose gladness they mingled, or woe;
The down-trampled thousands so quietly sleeping,
  Shrivelled to dust in the graveyard below:
Priest, learned doctor, grim lord of the manor,
  Damsel in kirtle, and furbelowed dame;
The knightly and noble, who bore on their banner
  Devices and mottoes emblazon'd to fame.

Mourn they full oft, in monotonous chiming,
  Hopes that were hallowed, or cherish'd, in vain ;
Of dreams rudely broken lamentingly rhyming ;
  Dreams made of melody, madness, and pain.
Often they tell of the miser, cold-hearted,
  Torn like a thief from his crime-gather'd gold ;
Mammon from money bags evermore parted ;
  Laid like a log in the pitiless mould.

Tolled they and chimed, in the days that are hoary,
  Days that are desolate, empty, and dead,
When abbey and priory flourished in glory,
  And matins were chanted, and masses were said.
Tolled they and chimed, to the seasons swift rolling,
  The spring-times, the summers, the autumns of old ;
The Yule-tides and Easters, God's people consoling ;
  The snow-shrouded winters, so dreary and cold.

Toll they, and chime they, to all generations;
Toll they, and chime, as the centuries flow :
Ring they, and sing they, with joy's gratulations;
Mourn they, and weep they, when joy is laid low.
Chiming and tolling ; rejoicing, repenting ;
Sadly, and gladly, to mortals they call :
Clear is their cadence, and sweet their lamenting ;
Mellow and mournful their harmonies fall.

# THE SINGER IN THE VALLEY.

One night, all faint and weary,
    I trod a lonely glen;
Dark was the way, and dreary,
    And far from homes of men.

The road lay black before me,
    No sound of life was heard;
An icy fear crept o'er me;
    My soul was terror-stirred.

A voice from the deep river
    Came moaning through the night:
I heard the great trees shiver,
    That crowned the gloomy height.

Ah then divinest music
    Brake softly on my ear;
A nightingale 'gan singing,
    Sweet, serene, and clear.

A song divine and tender,
    A pure, a holy lay,
A joy in the dark midnight,
    To cheer the lonely way.

Then too my heart was singing,
    As down the road I sped;
The path had now no terrors,
    For I was comforted.

## THE SINGER IN THE VALLEY.

And when I tread the valley,
    That lies in mortal shade,
Where the great world hath vanish'd,
    And vain all human aid:

Then may some holy angel
    Sing of the love divine:
There'll be no sweeter music
    To soothe this soul of mine.

E'en now, in care and sorrow,
    Storm-wearied, tempest-driven,
I hear thee in the darkness,
    Oh nightingale of heaven!

## THOU RENEWEST THE FACE OF THE EARTH.

Once more, my God, the world hath made
   Its old, old circuit round the sun;
   The everlasting seasons run;
Sunshine and splendour, gloom and shade.

Through the eternal years hast Thou
   The face of this great earth renew'd;
   Sequence of all vicissitude,
Thy past is present; future, now!

We cannot reach Thee; reason limps
  On broken crutches all the way:
  Thy light so great it darks our day:
We see thee, but with faintest glimpse.

For human sight is weak; the mind
  Strives to thine awful thought in vain:
  The dead weed floating on the main
As well might hope the stars to find.

Yet thou dost help us; thou hast rent
  The veil untouch'd by mortal power:
  On sea, on land,—on tree and flower,
Thy glory shineth: bloom and scent;

The morning, big with golden leaven;
  The slanting day-beam's sudden close,
  The yellow woods, the dying rose,
Are rich with thoughts of death and heaven.

Thou art the everlasting One,
   The great pervading Spirit, found
   In every place, and sight, and sound;
In heart and thought, in star and sun.

Not all that rash divines have preach'd;
   But something greater, something more
   Than sage of east or western lore,
Present or past, hath ever reach'd.

Wide is thy word: it may not be
   Set to vain fashions of the time:
   The solemn jest, the flippant rhyme,
Are not for that; are not for thee.

Only the earnest soul that seeks,
   By thee sustain'd, the upward path,
   And keepeth thy wise counsels, hath
The inner light that burns and breaks

With such a splendour on his way,
   He needs nor human torch nor spark;
   But through the mingled light and dark
Doth travel to the perfect day.

## THE SAXON RELIC IN ROMSEY ABBEY.

Saxon lady, once so fair;
Yet of whom the golden hair,
　Relic mute, alone is here:
As I pace my thoughtful way
Through the abbey quaint and grey;
　Organ-thunder pealing near;
　Music rolling on mine ear;
　Distant voices singing clear;
I to thee a pensive lay
Fain would dedicate to-day.

Since the first day thou wert dead,
Nine long centuries have fled :
Since those beauteous locks were
 braided,
What a wealth of love hath faded!
 Since last tears for thee were wept
 Many a dynasty hath swept
Spectral o'er th' historic page ;
King and statesman, poet, sage,
 Pope and prior, monk and priest,
 Haughty baron, belted knight,
Warrior peerless in the fight;
Minstrel gay, and lady bright;
 Courtly revel, royal feast ;
 All have vanished, all have ceased.


Earl's fair daughter; or, perchance,
Princess, for whom knightly lance

In war's mimicry was bent;
Who, at stately tournament,
Valour's prize awarded; gave
Wreaths and favours to the brave:
  Or, of some grim Saxon hold
  Light and idol, joy and pride;
Lily among thorns, like that
Long-wept maid of Astolat,
  Who for love of Lancelot died,
  Famed in legend sad and old.

Sorrow's tears for thee were shed,
  Falling bitter on thy breast,
When was laid that gentle head
  Low in its sepulchral rest:
Loving fingers wove the tresses
  Even Death was fain to spare:
O the kisses, the caresses
  Lavished on that golden hair.

Royal abbess, sainted nun
  Gathered, mourning, round thy
    grave:
  Down the long and stately nave,
When the funeral rites were done,
  Dirges for the fair and young
  In procession sad they sung.


Many a solemn mass was said;
Many a prayer for thee was prayed;
  Many a tale of thee was told
In those cloisters still and grey:
Oft the pilgrim, on his way
  To lone Warwell, or to old
Thuinam, or to Bewley's shrine,
Or Saint Mary's fane divine,
Spake of youth and beauty laid
Low in Romsey's hallow'd shade.

All have mouldered, one by one;
   Passing, with the passing time;
   Here a legend, there a rhyme;
Something suffer'd, said, or done.

Few the words, at most, and dim,
   That, half understood, remain;
   Sounding like a far-off strain
Of some long forgotten hymn.


Thus I muse as I behold,
   Far from worldly noise and stir,
These few gather'd locks of gold
   From a Saxon sepulchre;
Gleaming still with beauty rare,
Tresses of a lady's hair.

## TALK O' TH' HILL.

Sitting alone by a dying fire,
   I gaze on its ashes and silently muse :
I see there a city, a funeral pyre,
   A face that I lov'd, a man reading the news.

Sudden there leaps from the quivering flame,
   A mystical shape with a magical wand ;
I hear and obey, as he bids me by name,
   To look, and to listen, and understand.

And I see in a vision, between the bars,

    A thousand feet down to a desolate pit,

Where lamps dimly waver like tremulous stars,

    And the voices of many came up from it.

I see the red eyes of a demon glare,

    In a cavern of blackness crouching low;

His poisonous breath on the thickening air,

    Like an awful banner, waves to and fro.

Three hundred men of the village, I see,

    Strip to their labour, and work with a will;

And I know, as I look, that bread-winners they be,

    For the women and children of "Talk o' th' Hill."

The shout of the miner comes up from the deep,

    A song from those desolate dwellings of death;

A blow! the black walls crumble down in a heap,

    "Ho, ho!"—cries the miner—"'tis done!"—

    and takes breath.

Then out of the darkness a luminous ball
  Fierce flames through the pit with a blaze and a
    roar;
It licks up the strong men, who hurriedly call
  For help; and are silent, and dumb evermore.

For the demon rides swift in the strength of his
    wrath,
  With death on his breath, in the stroke of his
    hand:
The men of the village are swept from his path,
  And the wail of the widow is heard in the land.

And I knew as I look'd, that the vision was true:
  The spirit cried—"sing it!"  I answered—
    "I will!"
"Remember this Christmas,"—he said as he flew—
  "The widows and orphans at 'Talk o' th' Hill."

## NOT YET.

Dead snowdrop, slain by last night's frost;
Dishonour'd corse, whose silver head
And crown lies stained and tarnished,—
Its beauty gone, its glory lost,—
A sight for grief and love's regret,
That whispers to my heart—"not yet!"

The furze shows green along the hill,
Yet fears t' unfold her golden buds;

The bluebell, lady of the woods,
Lingers for sunshine, where the rill
Clamours till Spring's fair throne is set;
And waves cry to their weeds—"not yet!"


The primrose, darling of the vale,
Peeps shyly from her leafy sheath,
The great brown ragged oak beneath,
Whose bones are creaking in the gale:
The half-awaken'd violet
Starts up, and sighs—"not yet! not yet!"


Ah me! the nights are biting cold,
And winds are shrill, and skies are dark:
The dove, that flees from nature's ark,
May in such peril be too bold;
And fluttering, snared in danger's net,
May cry, when all too late—"not yet!"

## NOT YET.

Oh fair and perish'd child of earth,
In death so pure, so saintly sweet,
Old Winter weeps in rain and sleet,
The wreck of such untimely birth.
Gem, dropp'd from nature's coronet,
She sighs above thy grave—"not yet!"

Spring, gathering roses on her way,
Lingers in southern climes, and sings;
And listening to sweet-voiced strings
Of love and gladness, doth delay
Her coming; keeps the year in debt;
And answers to our prayer—"not yet!"

So love's fair bloom, by fate unkind,
Like thee, sweet flower, too oft must fade,
And sinks forgotten in the shade
Of death, that creepeth care behind.
Ah life is but one long regret;
And hope can only sigh—"not yet!"

# THE HOUSE MINSTREL.

Sweet bird, that singest in thy cage,
   A prisoner all the year;
I look up from my ledger's page,
   Well pleased thy voice to hear.

A sprig of garden weed, a drink
   Of water, daily given,
Fresh seed, clean gravel, are, I think,
   To thee like joys of heaven.

For thou thy little throat dost clear
    With such a sweet rejoice,
That all the world is fain to hear
    The music of thy voice.

Why should I play so weak a part,
    And give to fortune blame,
When thou dost keep so blithe a heart
    In such a tiny frame?

Thou singest, let it rain or shine,
    Or bright the day, or dull:
Thy little soul with joy divine,
    O'erflows, it is so full.

While I, immersed in mean affairs,
    Through life but seem to crawl,
Snail-like, and loaded with such cares,
    I scarce can sing at all.

And when my soul doth sing with thine,
   So poor I deem the strain,
I would all minstrelsy resign,
   To thee, nor sing again.

Hast thou no longing to be free,
   To break thy prison bars,
And wing thy way o'er land and sea,
   May be, among the stars?

Are there no dreams of thine that speak
   Of ocean's breezy miles,
Where Teneriffe lifts his cloudy peak,
   Lord of the lonely isles:

Where the bright southern waters lave
   The land of happy calms,
And tropic bowers of beauty wave,
   In shade of giant palms.

I too a captive am, confined
    To labour's weary oar,
To keep with toil of heart and mind
    Misfortune from the door.

Like thee a prisoner, shut in
    A somewhat wider cage;
But sick and sadden'd with the din
    Of this relentless age.

Oh for the pleasant days to be!
    By care no more distrest;
When, like a bird, my soul shall flee
    Away, and be at rest.

'Tis base to murmur and repine,
    As one whom fortune cows;
I'll keep a heart as sound as thine,
    Sweet minstrel of the house!

## ELLEN SOMERS.

You will see my face no more;
      Ellen Somers!
You for me may close the door.
Sweep the traces from the floor
Steps of mine have made. I swore
Last night, from my bosom's core,
So to sweep you evermore:
      Ellen Somers!

False and fickle you may be;
: Ellen Somers!
Fickle as the summer sea;
Or the lights that come and flee
In April, over hill and lea:
False and fickle unto me
You shall never, never be;
: Ellen Somers!


Take the ribbon, and the ring;
: Ellen Somers!
Take this rose—a faded thing;
Take the song I heard you sing
A night you know of in the spring.
Back with scorn to you I fling
Song and ribbon, rose and ring;
: Ellen Somers!

## THE PESTILENCE.

The heavy air with pestilence is laden :
   A nameless horror hangs about the street :
There are no greetings now 'tween youth and maiden :
   And business shuffles by on frightened feet.

Death slinks, and hides in crevices and corners,
   An ambushed tiger, waiting for the leap :
All day the bell tolls; but there are no mourners;
   When all fear death, who for the dead shall weep ?

A look of fear lies on the very houses ;
 Their walls are whispering dreadful messages
Of ghastly bridals, where the worm espouses
 The beauty that we lov'd, and taints the breeze.

Like fate the clouds hang, low, and dark, and leaden :
 The sun, as when on that Egyptian day,
He troubled Pharoah and his host, doth redden
 With anger, sending forth his shafts to slay.

The wind about the city wanders slowly :
 The streets are dropping with its heavy breath :
The river, musical and melancholy,
 Is dirging to the sea a dirge of death.

The meadows, daisy-pied, and green and golden,
 Are lonely ; for the children that did run
Among them, with their mothers closely folden
 In earth are lying, hidden from the sun.

Slowly the night comes,—shadowy, black, and
    solemn:
The footfalls of the morning are not heard:
The ivy trembles above cross and column,
    Where grave-grown grasses by the breeze are
    stirr'd.


The day is full of grief and mortal losses;
    The graves are choking with their tenants
    dreary;
The doors are painted thick with bloody crosses,
    And labelled with a mournful *miserere!*


The eye of man is cruel to his brother;
    For life than love is more, and more than gain;
A selfish fear all nobleness doth smother;
    The pestilence hath smitten love in twain.

O thou who rulest in the heav'nly city,
   Lift from the world thy sin-avenging rod!
Lord we have wander'd from thee; let thy pity
   Listen, and save, and bring us back to God.

## THE CAPTAIN'S WIFE.

Oh mighty wind that bloweth :
Oh tempest strong that goeth
In paths no mortal knoweth :
   King of the viewless air !
The wild, wild waters sweeping ;
The waves in mountains heaping ;
List to my bitter weeping,—
   List to my lonely pray'r !

Oppress'd with fear and wonder,
I hear thy voice of thunder ;
Oh part us not asunder :

My laddie's on the sea.
Oh work him no disaster ;
But faster, wind ! and faster,
The good ship and her master,
   Bring, bring them back to me.

Think, in thy dreadful rages,
Of infants' helpless ages,
Of men that sail for wages,
   Of one who sails for me :
And bid the stormy waters
Cease from their cruel slaughters,
That sailors' wives and daughters
   No more may weep for thee.

Last night I lay a dreaming,
My heart with sad thoughts teeming ;
I heard the tempest screaming ;
   I heard the ocean roar.

I dreamt a death-gun's booming
Came out of the deep glooming,
My winsome laddie dooming
    To darkness evermore.


I woke: the lattice paning
Was quivering and complaining:
The blowing and the raining
    Fill'd my poor heart with fear.
My babe—some care possessed her:
Close to my love I press'd her;
I kiss'd her lips and bless'd her;
    And prayed for Willie dear.

        .

What's this? oh joy! a letter!
'Tis Willie's hand! ah better!
He's landed! I'm your debtor,
    Good postman; here's your fee.

Thanks, wind! that no disaster
Didst bring; but faster, faster,
The good ship and her master
　Hast thus brought back to me.

# THE WRECK OF THE "LONDON."

Down the bright Solent Sea,
   The steamer "London" came;
A stately sight to see;
   A ship of goodly fame.
For Sydney bound was she:
   "Martin," the captain's name.

Brave men were all her crew,
   Used round the world to roam:
Tried was each man, and true,
   And bronz'd with sun and foam:

On waters wide and blue
  They made their floating home.

From Plymouth's stormy bay,
  The sixth day of the year,
The "London" ploughed her way,
  Freighted with friends most dear.
Few thoughts of grief had they :
  Their spirits knew no fear.

Two days at sea : the skies
  Have angry grown, and dark :
The bellowing tempest flies ;
  Gloom gathers round the bark ;
Waves that in mountains rise,
  Sore toss the labouring ark.

Wildly the tempests sweep,
  Her deck from stem to stern ;

The lions of the deep
  Their rage upon her turn:
And mothers learn to weep,
  And babes in wonder mourn.


Two days in terror's shade,
  For life they laboured on:
Stoutly they toil'd and prayed,
  Till strength and hope had gone:
Then bent their heads and said,—
  "O Lord thy will be done."


Thus by the tempest's spite,
  And ocean's cruel pride,
In an unequal fight,
  Good seamanship was tried.
"Science and human might
  Are vain!"—the captain cried.

Then godly preachers knelt
  With passengers and crew;
And stony hearts did melt,
  As heav'n came into view:
In such dread hour was felt
  What a true man may do.


The captain his brave head
  Bared, with all manhood crown'd;
And manly words were said,
  With mighty thoughts profound:
The "service for the dead"
  Uprose with solemn sound.


A mighty billow rolled
  Athwart the broken ship;
The bells of ocean tolled,
  As, with a sudden dip,

With life, and goods, and gold,
   She sank in death's rude grip.

Three hundred souls that day,—
   Friends, parents, children fair,—
To stormy deeps a prey,
   Went down with psalm and
      prayer;
God with them all the way;
   Unseen, but truly there,

Thanks to the gracious power
   That, while it did not save,
Made them in such an hour
   So calm, so grandly brave:
And gave, as manhood's dower
   This tale of wind and wave.

# THE FOREST NOOK

The nook lies deep in woods, where three brooks
    meet,
And make a little river, that doth run
Westward for ever, winding with the sun,
Twirling gay bells of silver round the feet
Of listening willows; on its breast a fleet
Of new-dropt blossoms, scenting all the air
With summer odours: tiny surges beat
On golden shallows, musical and fair.

Here doth the sedge its long green banners wave
Above the water-violets pale and rare;
And blue forget-me-nots and maiden-hair
Frolic with celandine and meadow-sweet;
And here the lady lily, pure and grave,
Doth her dear face in coolest waters lave.


Let us rest here, in summer's silent noon,
In sweet seclusion, far from men and books,
Forgetting for a time the cranks and crooks
Of fortune; gladden'd with the pleasant tune
Of water, and the lulling of the leaves,
And laughter of the lazy winds of June.
Behold! around us the great forest heaves
Cathedral aisles of foliage, vistas dim
Receding into distance, arches high
And awful, many-columned; bough and limb
Stretch'd in a mighty roof athwart the sky:

The giant trunks take mystic shapes and grim,—
Druidic monsters; one might fancy Eve's
Old Paradise were here, and Adam somewhere
    nigh.

It is the voice of God among the trees:
The wind is rising, and doth strongly shake
The temple of his glory, and doth make
A sound like to the roaring of the seas,
As if innumerable majesties
Were passing all unseen through the great woods;
Unseen, but not unfelt: the solitudes
Thrill with the wondrous presence drawing near.
How dreadful is this place! Lo, He is here,
Holding a court of sylvan state—the Lord
Whom angels serve, men worship, demons fear.
Let us go hence, and seek the lonely grot,
That lieth yonder, opposite the ford:
This ground is holy, and we knew it not.

# THE GRAVE BY THE RIVER.

In a valley green and deep,
  By a river tenanted,
Where bright waters flash and sweep,
  And the sunset falleth red;
Where the shading willows weep,
  And the lily makes her bed;
There the minstrel sleeps the sleep
  Of the dead.

Music of the sobbing stream
    Mourning ever round his grave,
He doth hear, as in a dream:
    Sweet, the ever-singing wave,
Lulls the poet-heart to rest,
Where the birds have built their nest
    In the sunny branches spread
    Overhead.

Lo! the scented summer breeze
    Slowly sailing, moving by,
Doth awaken in the trees
    Half a murmur, half a sigh:
And, a mile away, the surf
    Falling idly on the shore,
Dimly soundeth, where the turf,
Lying green upon his breast,
Laps him in a peaceful rest,
    Evermore!

## THE GRAVE BY THE RIVER.

Sleep, oh Singer, in thy vale!
  Crimsom day-beams dying, fall
Round thee; and the nightingale
  Calleth, with a silver call,
To her mate within the woods.
  Peaceful, by the quiet wave,
Where no mortal foot intrudes,
  Is thy grave!

Thou shalt have no burial stone,
  Speaking carven words of thee:
Turf shall mark thy place alone
  By the river, where the bee
Sings of thee with ceaseless drone,
In a mellow monotone;
And the stream doth make a moan
  To the wind and to the sea,
For the something that is gone,
  That was Thee!

## THE SEER.

In Patmos' isle of revelation, John
  The lov'd apostle, saw a heavenly sight,
And heard, while the ineffable glory shone,
  A voice, as of one talking, saying —" Write
  The things that thou hast seen!" So in the night
Of this mortality, the poet sees
  A heaven above him, and a golden door
  Thrown wide, and henceforth issuing evermore,
Trains of sublimest thoughts, and imageries
  Holy and wonderful; and voices greet
Him from the temple-altars, far and dim—
  "Sing that which God hath shewn thee, as is meet
To thine own soul,—in epic, song, or hymn:
  The world shall hear, and deem the music sweet!"

LYMINGTON:

PRINTED BY HENRY DOMAN, BOOKSELLER AND STATIONER,

HIGH STREET.

www.ingramcontent.com/pod-product-compliance
Lightning Source LLC
Chambersburg PA
CBHW032228230426
43666CB00033B/1636